D0908681

Shippensburg Public Library
73 West King Street
Shippensburg, PA 17257
717-532-4508

Animals with Jobs

Guide Dogs

Judith Janda Presnall

KidHaven Press, an imprint of Gale Group, Inc.
10911 Technology Place, San Diego, CA 92127

For the loving, caring puppy raisers.

Library of Congress Cataloging-in-Publication Data
Presnall, Judith Janda.
    Guide dogs / by Judith Janda Presnall
        p. cm. — (Animals with jobs)
    Includes bibliographical references and index.
    Summary: Discusses guide dogs, their selection and training, the
preferred breeds, and their work with the vision-impaired.
    ISBN 0-7377-0935-9 (hardback : alk. paper)
    1. Guide dogs 2. Dog trainers. [1. Guide dogs. 2. Dogs.] I. Title
II. Series
    HV1780 .P74 2002
    636.7'0886—dc21

                                                      2001000847

Acknowledgments

    I would like to thank the following people who joyfully and expertly
reviewed my manuscript:

- Rhonda Bissell, tour director at Guide Dogs of America in Sylmar,
  California. Rhonda has also raised two GDA puppies.
- Jolie Mason, who has had her guide dog, Yuma, since 1990.
- Louise Nicholson, Jolie's sister, who read the manuscript to Jolie.
- Linda Vieira, puppy raiser for Guide Dogs of America.

Copyright © 2002 by KidHaven Press, an imprint of Gale Group, Inc.
10911 Technology Place, San Diego, CA 92127

No part of this book may be reproduced or used in any form or by any other
means, electrical, mechanical, or otherwise, including, but not limited to,
photocopying, recording, or any information storage and retrieval system,
without prior written permission from the publisher.

Printed in the U.S.A.

Contents

Chapter One

Partners Who Change Lives

Aguide dog serves as a partner for a person who is blind or has limited vision. Serving as the partner's eyes, the guide dog provides the partner with **independence** and **mobility**.

Many people who cannot see are unable to leave their homes without a friend or relative to escort them. They cannot drive. They cannot walk across streets or even find curbs. Guide dogs help their partners move safely through traffic and around **obstacles**.

Unlike a human escort, the dog is available at all times. The sight-**impaired** person no longer has to call on anyone to take him or her to the store, the bank, or for a walk.

Guide Dogs Give Freedom

One young woman, Toni, felt restricted in her mobility and independence. Toni had been blind since birth. Although she was skillful at using a cane, she found it difficult to use a cane and wheel a stroller when her first baby was born. She applied to Guide Dogs of

A guide dog tours with a partner who is blind.

America in Sylmar, California, for a guide dog. She was partnered with a female yellow Labrador retriever named Clancy. Now Toni walks her three children to school each morning and brings them home safely every afternoon. If she needs something from the store, she does not have to wait for her husband to come home. She makes the trip with Clancy and her kids.

Toni says, "Clancy is a great companion. She's wonderful with my children. She loves to play. But put the harness on and she's all business. She's great. What I love about having Clancy is that my husband doesn't have to do everything. I can do my share. I can be involved in my kids' schools. I'm not stuck at home, and neither are the kids. We go to the playground and Clancy helps by following the kids. It's hard to imagine life without her."[1]

Like Toni, Jolie Mason found the use of a cane to sometimes be slow and tedious. Jolie, who is now totally blind, used a cane for eight years before getting a guide dog. She explains the difference a dog has made

Guide Dogs Welcome Here

Access laws in the United States and Canada, including the Americans With Disabilities Act, permit guide dogs and their handlers to go everywhere the general public is allowed:

🐾 stores
🐾 restaurants
🐾 office buildings
🐾 taxis
🐾 buses
🐾 trains and airplanes
🐾 all areas of public accommodation

A guide dog is trained to stand, sit, or lie quietly in public places when not leading.

Source: Guide Dogs for the Blind, Inc.

Jolie Mason enjoys a cup of coffee. Guide dog Yuma lies at her feet.

in her life. "When I had my cane and I wanted to leave a room, I would tap my way to the back of the room until I hit a wall. Then I would turn left or right and walk along that wall, tapping until I felt either another wall or an opening. After I got my black Labrador, Yuma, I would just say, 'Yuma, find the door,' and she would guide me straight to the door."[2]

Guiding Through Traffic

When outdoors, a guide dog leads the partner safely around obstacles and across busy streets.

A guide dog is trained to protect its human partner from the hazards of traffic. However, the dog cannot tell red lights from green lights. Nor can the dog read stop signs. The sight-impaired person must listen to the flow of traffic, decide when it is safe, and give the command "Forward!" But it is not always safe. Sometimes, the person makes a mistake.

Stephen Kuusisto once had this experience. Stephen was born with partial sight. He can see a little, but not well enough to read an ordinary book or drive a car.

Once when Stephen and his dog Corky were standing at a curb in White Plains, New York, the dog suddenly

A guide dog responds to a "forward" command given by its partner.

Stopping at a curb, a guide dog alerts its partner to the coming step down.

and strongly jerked Stephen straight back from the curb. Corky had seen a Jeep that was coming close to the concrete edging. Because Stephen was unaware of the approaching Jeep, Corky's alertness to this hazard avoided a possible disaster.

Guiding Around Obstacles

Hazards abound on city streets for people with limited vision. Curbs and stairs offer two examples. It is the job of

9

A woman walks safely around a tree with the help of her guide dog.

the guide dog to stop at all curbs and stairs. This is a signal to the partner that he or she needs to step up or down. The dogs also guide their charges around other obstacles.

Jolie Mason says, "When Yuma and I walk in parks, Yuma always keeps me on the path. She guides me around all the flower gardens, bushes, and trees. I never have to worry about colliding with people, either. When I had my cane, I would have never considered going outside for a walk for fun. I tended to spend my time either at work or in my home."[3]

Sighted people move out of the way of **pedestrians** and bicyclists. Sighted people walk around deep holes. They see curbs and steps. Guide dogs see these obstacles for their partners. Many times, the partner is unaware of what the dog has avoided. Sometimes, a passerby or instructor will tell the dog's partner.

Andy Potok and his dog Dash, a black male German shepherd, were in training class at The Seeing Eye in Morristown, New Jersey, when such an episode occurred. Andy tells the story: "[Walking really fast] along South Street, Dash comes to a stop at a car blocking the sidewalk. 'Hup, up,' I tell him, in this case meaning, 'Find your way carefully past this obstacle.' Slowly, he begins to take me around the rear of the car. Suddenly he jerks me backward, his body taut and watchful. Behind me, [my instructor], like a proud mother, tells me what had just happened. Apparently a plume of exhaust in [Dash's] face warned my wonderful dog that the car was about to back up."[4] Such tasks are all in a day's work for a guide dog.

Chapter Two

The Qualified Guide Dog

The most important characteristics of a guide dog are alertness, intelligence, and willingness to learn. Dogs must be alert and intelligent to make life-saving decisions. The dog must also enjoy working with people.

A good partnership depends on confidence and trust. While still at Guiding Eyes for the Blind training school in Yorktown Heights, New York, Stephen Kuusisto discovered Corky's instinct for protecting him from hazards. Corky was smart enough to know when it was not safe to obey a command. On a White Plains railroad station platform, Corky, Stephen, and a trainer, Kathy, waited on the elevated edge for a train. Kathy wanted to prove to Stephen that he could have complete confidence in Corky and that the dog was intelligent enough to know when to be stubborn and disobey.

Kathy told Stephen to give Corky the "forward" command. Stephen was afraid because of the long drop to the tracks below. Hesitantly, Stephen finally gave the

A guide dog waits for a command from its partner.

command, hoping Corky would not obey. Corky yanked Stephen backward, then turned and walked him in the opposite direction until they were safely away from the tracks. After this episode, Stephen felt assured of Corky's abilities.

Stephen described his feelings about his dog: "Guide dogs become partners who make intelligent judgments for you throughout the day, that preserve and protect your freedom of movement and safety."[5]

The Best Breeds

Experience has shown that golden retrievers, Labrador retrievers, and German shepherds make the best guide dogs. These breeds are gentle but strong. They are obedient, but also will disobey a command if they see danger. Both male and female dogs work equally well.

Guide dogs must be medium size in order to fit under restaurant tables or under bus, train, or airplane seats. Dogs that are twenty to twenty-eight inches tall at the shoulders and that weigh about fifty pounds are ideal. This size allows the dog to keep up with a walking partner. A smaller dog would have to walk too fast and thus would tire easily.

Guide dog schools have found that the best way to obtain dogs with these characteristics is to **breed** them. At Guide Dogs for the Blind in San Rafael, California, about 150 dogs are bred each year for guide dog work. At any given time, the school may have more than 300 dogs in some stage of training.

The Puppy Stage

Puppies remain at the school until they are between six and eleven weeks old. At that time, they are given to a prescreened foster family. While with that family, the puppy undergoes obedience training and learns to be around people. How well the puppy learns during this time will decide whether it goes on to guide dog training. The foster family provides the care and activities that are necessary for the development of a future guide dog. But one person in the family, usually a child or teenager, has the primary responsibility for the pup's daily care and routine.

Members of the 4-H Club often raise guide dog puppies. Children nine years old and above who are

A sight-impaired traveler and his dog explore their surroundings.

4-H members can participate with their parents' permission. The puppy raisers will take care of the dog for about fifteen months. They teach the dog general obedience, such as how to sit, stay, lie down, fetch, come on command, and walk on a leash.

Training a Puppy

Training begins immediately. The **foster parent housebreaks** the puppy by following a regular schedule of taking the dog outside. Twelve-year-old George, who is a 4-H Club member raising a guide dog puppy in

A puppy-in-training takes a well-deserved rest.

Hackettstown, New Jersey, told his classmates how he housebreaks his puppy, Doug: "Every day I take him to the same spot for him to go to the bathroom. The trainers call it 'emptying.' Then at night I put a short leash on him and tie him to the front of my bed. He won't empty where he sleeps, so if he wants to go, he'll make a racket and wake me up. I jump up and rush him outside to the spot where he's supposed to go. The short leash also trains him to stay beside the master's bed in case the blind person needs him in the middle of the night."[6]

The puppy also needs to be taught other forms of good household behavior. Foster families provide the puppy with chew toys since puppies love to exercise their jaws and teeth. However, if the puppy chews on furniture, shoes, slippers, or carpets, the dog must be disciplined with a firm voice—not by hitting or shouting. When the puppy's actions are acceptable, the dog is rewarded with verbal praise and stroking.

Behaving

Another job for the puppy raiser is to make sure that the puppy learns how to behave around people and in public places. This is called "**socialization**." Whether it is a short trip to the store, a long vacation across the country, or even a ride in a little red wagon, each outing prepares the puppy for its future travels as a guide dog. The foster family will take the puppy to many activities and to a variety of locations, including shops, parks, and playgrounds. Riding on buses, subways, and trains is also part of the training.

The puppy must learn how to behave in a noisy, active world in order to become a guide dog. Walks on city streets familiarize the dog with traffic. Foster parents also introduce a puppy to routine household noises such as vacuum cleaners and fans. In addition, the puppy is exposed to distracting noises (such as applause and the clatter of construction sites) and to different scents (like those found in a pet store). The dog learns how to be well behaved despite **distractions**. All of these

Chew toys help puppies exercise their jaws and teeth.

Guide dogs learn to ignore distractions such as traffic noise when walking outside.

indoor and outdoor experiences help prepare the dog for a future role as a guide dog.

It is important to teach the dog to ignore distractions. At a guide dog school event, puppy raisers tested the dogs by having them walk through an obstacle course. The puppies had to pass hot dogs hanging from strings, a noisy shopping cart, a caged pig, a squawking chicken, and the roaring engine of a Harley Davidson motorcycle. If a dog stopped to sniff or jump, more work lay ahead.

When the dog is about eighteen months old, the foster family returns the puppy to the guide dog school for formal training. About 60 percent of the puppies that reach this stage are rejected as unsuitable for further training. Those that are nervous, easily distracted, or fearful are returned to the puppy raiser or given to some other qualified person.

If there is doubt about a puppy's ability, a trainer may have to look more carefully at the puppy's behavior.

Mari, a guide dog trainer at Guide Dogs of America, told of her experience with a puppy named Tyler. "Tyler was well-trained by his puppy raiser foster family, but I think he was just born with a zany streak. For example, on his first day back at guide dog school, he jumped over the couch and onto the coffee table! He

A hot dog is a strong lure for a puppy-in-training.

Puppies love to chew on things, even faces.

was silly and rowdy. And, just like any class clown, he got all the other dogs in trouble with his antics and teasing. . . . I would have 'expelled' this clown from guide dog school, except for one very important thing. As soon as the harness was on, he was a different dog— and one of the hardest workers I've ever trained."[7]

Training to Become a Partner

Guide dog training is a two-step process. The first step lasts four to six months with a trained instructor. The second step starts when the dog is assigned to its future partner. The pair trains for four weeks. If the dog and partner successfully complete the training, they go home to a new life together.

During the formal training, dogs learn to respond intelligently to changes in their surroundings. They are taught to lead their partners rather than to walk in a heel position. Gradually, the dogs learn to assume responsibility and make sure that their human partners travel safely.

A trainer begins by teaching the dog commands such as "forward," "left," "right," and "halt." The dog wears a harness with a tall handle, which the instructor holds. The commands are learned by repetition, and the dog is rewarded with verbal encouragement, such as "good dog," and pats on the head when each command is done correctly. This training takes place on the school grounds until the dog has mastered the commands.

Since the trainer can see, the trainer teaches the dog to go around obstacles by commanding "left" and "right." He or she also teaches the dog to stop at curbs and steps—up or down—by commanding "halt." When the dog is ready to leave the campus, the trainer will first work with the dog in a **residential** neighborhood, stopping at curbs and following "right" and "left" commands. From there, the training session moves to an area where traffic is heavier and there are more pedestrians. The team crosses streets and walks around obstacles.

The dog advances to the next training stage by going to malls and buildings, where the dog is trained to enter elevators and revolving doors. The dog also learns to take a partner up and down stairs. When the dog is skilled at leading the trainer in this area, they head downtown to train, where traffic is most **congested**.

Trainers work with guide dogs at a subway terminal.

The final test requires the trainer to wear a blindfold and walk with the dog in a busy downtown neighborhood. A dog that shows it can enter elevators, travel up and down steps, go through revolving doors, cross busy streets, stay calm around loud noises, and obey commands is ready for a sight-impaired partner.

Partner Assignments

Trainers try to match people with the dogs that best fit their needs. Because Jolie Mason is slightly over five feet

During training, a guide dog wears a harness with a tall handle.

A woman and her dog walk confidently through a maze of poles as part of their training.

tall, the trainers paired her with Yuma, who weighed about fifty-five pounds. Bigger dogs have much more strength and would pull Jolie to a "gallop" down the street. Yuma also had to be flexible in new situations and like people because Jolie traveled on an airplane about twice a month and her job required her to be around many people. Yuma's puppy raiser was a school-teacher, and the dog had spent much time around children in her classroom.

Once a dog is paired with its partner, the two will live together in a dormitory room on the campus of the guide dog school. The dog must learn to obey commands from this new person. To win the dog's loyalty, the new partner takes over the feeding, grooming, and exercising of the dog. Partner-training at the school lasts twenty-eight days. During training, an instructor goes everywhere with the new team. The instructors make sure that the partners **communicate** with each other. The new handler must get used to having a dog guide him or her. Students practice commands. During their daily five-mile walks, the partners work on developing a close relationship with each other.

For the next month, the group of up to twenty-four students and their dogs eat their meals in the school cafeteria. Even mealtime provides an opportunity for

A guide dog provides freedom for a partner to walk anywhere.

By law, guide dogs are allowed in all stores.

training. If the dogs try to chew on the chair rungs or get playful with each other, the students must command "No!" and give a short downward jerk to the dog's leash to remind the dogs to behave.

The Final Week

By the fourth week, students are ready to try to put what they have learned to use. The trainers take the partners by vans to a quiet residential area to practice what they have learned. Later, the teams go to busier parts of town. The training can sometimes be hard and even scary.

Andy Potok explains the panic and pain he felt on one outing: "When Dash smacks me head-on into a parking meter, I am furious, indignant, as well as bloodied. As hard as it has been for most of us to exercise leash corrections properly, not wanting to hurt our precious dogs, I now wish that my left arm were made

Guide dogs and their partners need at least one year to form a good team.

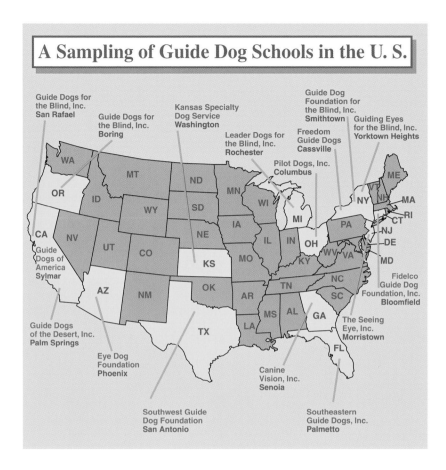

A Sampling of Guide Dog Schools in the U. S.

Guide Dogs for the Blind, Inc.
San Rafael

Guide Dogs for the Blind, Inc.
Boring

Kansas Specialty Dog Service
Washington

Leader Dogs for the Blind, Inc.
Rochester

Guide Dog Foundation for the Blind, Inc.
Smithtown

Freedom Guide Dogs
Cassville

Guiding Eyes for the Blind, Inc.
Yorktown Heights

Pilot Dogs, Inc.
Columbus

Guide Dogs of America
Sylmar

Guide Dogs of the Desert, Inc.
Palm Springs

Eye Dog Foundation
Phoenix

Southwest Guide Dog Foundation
San Antonio

Canine Vision, Inc.
Senoia

Southeastern Guide Dogs, Inc.
Palmetto

The Seeing Eye, Inc.
Morristown

Fidelco Guide Dog Foundation, Inc.
Bloomfield

of steel. I want to hurt him. 'How could you do this to me?' I scream. 'Do you call this ***bonding***, you miserable cur [mongrel dog]?' . . . Five blocks later, as Dash stops neatly at a curb, my praise sounds thin and phony. I am still furious. The instructor explains to me that Dash has no idea why I am still angry. [The instructor] tells me to forget my anger right after I correct."[8]

After all the required training is completed, the students do a test walk. Each dog-and-student team is sent out alone to cover a route outlined in advance. The team must cross a number of light-controlled streets, board a bus for a brief ride, go to a specific store and buy something, and then return to the school. An instructor silently trails the team.

The final phase is graduation day, when the guide dog is formally certified. Each year, approximately thirteen hundred teams graduate from the fourteen guide dog schools in the United States.

After graduating from Guide Dogs for the Blind in San Rafael, California, one student, Belveia Benzenhafer, was asked how she felt about her future. She answered, "Sad. Happy. Scared. Excited. All of these. It will be such a miracle to go places on my own without asking someone to take me. Thanks to [my golden retriever] Cindy, I can even go away to college, and my family won't have to worry about me."[9]

Chapter Four

Going Home

The first six months at home are the most crucial in any guide dog partnership. During that time, the dog and person must build on the relationship that began at the school.

Many lives will be changed, especially those of the family who have always helped the family member who is blind. One school sends a letter to the family advising them on proper homecoming behavior: "Keep emotions down on arrival, greet the dog quietly, [and] do not follow the team down the street to see how [they] work."[10]

New Challenges

Some guide dogs arrive at their new home to find other pets in the household. This can be challenging for everyone. Pets, such as cats, keep the family on their toes until the household settles down.

The handler must be firm with the new partner. If the dog misbehaves, such as putting its paws on the

A guide dog (right) must adjust to other family pets.

counter, chasing a cat, barking, or growling, for example, it must be reprimanded by a jerk of the leash and a firm "No!" command.

It is not always easy to have everything work as smoothly as it did at the school. For example, Andy Potok had problems soon after he arrived home: "I find I tend to let Dash get away with minor infractions, such as a semi-protective growl or two, or a turning of his head to check whether [my wife] is still walking with us. At a small local restaurant, I'm having too nice a

Guide dogs quickly learn their partner's daily route and workplace.

time to notice that my guide dog has wandered over to the next table, just to be friendly. After three months my permissiveness has created [a difficult] situation. Dash is now easily distracted, restless, on edge."[11] Often, the student will call the school and have an instructor come out to help him or her reestablish obedience rules.

The new handler must win the dog's affection or the partnership will fail. A routine must be established quickly. For example, the human partner must form mental maps of his or her neighborhood and work-place. The person must know how many streets to cross, where to wait for the bus, and how far to walk after getting off the bus. After being directed with com-mands, the dog quickly learns the daily route and workplace, and learns to connect names with places.

Sheila Hocken of Nottingham, England, describes her experience with her chocolate-brown Labrador, Emma, after about two years of partnership. "Emma quickly learned the names of all the shops and bus sta-tions I used. . . . Emma was quite amazing. Her mind was an encyclopedia of shops' names. I would have only to say the word and we were there, with never a mistake or hesitation, through the mill of other shoppers and the various tempting smells."[12]

Guide Dogs at Play and at Work

To make sure that loyalty remains with the dog's part-ner, family **interaction** with the dog must be limited. The dog's partner is responsible for exercise, feeding, and grooming. The dog's friendship develops because

A family member enjoys a guide dog.

of the dog's dependence on the partner for its care. The person trusts the dog, and the dog trusts the person. However, when the dog is out of its harness, it is treated like any other pet. The guide dog is treated like a member of the family. It lives indoors and sleeps in its partner's bedroom on the floor next to the bed.

Guide dogs in harness are working. They should not be offered food or toys, or be petted without permission. Petting a guide dog distracts it from its work. The dog may think it is playtime and have trouble getting back to work.

When seventeen-year-old Hayley completed training with her black lab, Casper, she fretted about bringing her dog to school. "At first I was really worried that everyone at school would try to pet him, and wouldn't listen when I told them not to," Hayley says. "But from the first day, it was really great. Lots of times now, when people see one of their friends going to pet Casper, they tell them, 'No, you can't pet that dog.' It's worked out really, really well."[13]

Retiring a Guide Dog

Most guide dogs retire at age ten. Old age, hip problems, and other common dog ailments make it hard for a dog to keep working. Often, the retired dog goes to live with relatives or friends of the guide dog user. However, if this is not possible, the school finds a home for it.

Etiquette and the Visually Impaired

DO	DON'T
Speak in a normal tone of voice.	Speak loudly or shout.
Talk directly to a blind person.	Speak to a blind person by addressing his companion.
Address blind people by name, so they know that you are speaking to them.	Enter or leave a room without advising the person.
Leave doors and cupboards fully open or completely closed, so they do not become obstacles to a blind person.	Rearrange furniture or personal belongings. Blind people rely on knowing where things are.
Understand that only the blind person must give commands to his or her guide dog.	Try to assist a blind person without asking their permission.

Guide Dogs for the Blind, Inc.

Guide dogs are loyal, trusting, and dependable.

Parting is not easy. Both dog and person often feel the loss. One young woman, Deborah Groeber, said her yellow Labrador retriever, Bonnie, developed hip problems when she was only eight. At times, Bonnie would simply stop and refuse to walk. Frightened for her dog, Deborah turned to Guiding Eyes for the Blind, where she had obtained Bonnie. The school told her it was time for Bonnie to retire. The trainer suggested that

Sometimes both husband and wife have guide dogs.

Deborah's parents take Bonnie. Devastated, Deborah called a friend. "I don't know what to do. . . . What do people do in my situation? Bonnie's not just a dog. She's part of me."[14]

Hard as it was, Deborah packed up Bonnie's things, bought her favorite dog food, and took the dog to her parents' home. Bonnie was familiar with her new home since she had spent vacations with Deborah's parents.

Within six weeks, Deborah had trained a new dog, a two-year-old black Labrador named Duncan. When Deborah and the new dog visited her parents, Bonnie leapt into the air as soon as she saw Deborah. When Deborah got the harness to take Duncan for a walk, Bonnie raced to try to get into it. With a shaky voice, Deborah grasped Bonnie's smooth head and told the dog, "I love you, Bonnie, but it's time for us both to move on. . . . Go with Mom."[15] Her mother gently pulled the dog away.

Gifts of Life

Guide dogs are gifts, allowing a blind person to live a life of independence and to live it with dignity. They are one-half of a partnership built on trust and dependability. Once a sight-impaired person has a guide dog, he or she cannot imagine life without one. The guide dog links a partner who is blind to the seeing world.

Notes

Chapter One: Partners Who Change Lives

1. Quoted in an undated letter from Guide Dogs of America.
2. Interview with Jolie Mason, January 2001.
3. Interview with Jolie Mason, January 2001.
4. Andrew Potok, "Dash and Me," *Life*, July 1988, p. 78.

Chapter Two: The Qualified Guide Dog

5. Quoted in Sherry Bennett Warshauer, *Everyday Heroes: Extraordinary Dogs Among Us.* New York: Howell Book House, 1998, p. 34.
6. Quoted in Susan Kuklin, *Mine for a Year.* New York: Coward-McCann, 1984, p. 27.
7. Quoted in an undated letter from Guide Dogs of America.

Chapter Three: Training to Become a Partner

8. Potok, "Dash and Me," pp. 75, 78.
9. Quoted in Elizabeth Simpson Smith, *A Guide Dog Goes to School.* New York: William Morrow, 1987, p. 46.

Chapter Four: Going Home

10. Potok, "Dash and Me," p. 78.
11. Potok, "Dash and Me," p. 78.
12. Sheila Hocken, "Emma and I," *Good Housekeeping,* March 1978, p. 175.
13. Quoted in *Guide Dogs of America Partners,* "Casper: High School Hero!" Winter 1998, p. 1.
14. Quoted in Anita Bartholomew, "A Perfect Match," *Reader's Digest,* September 1996, p. 89.
15. Quoted in Bartholomew, "A Perfect Match," p. 90.

Glossary

bond: To become closer to someone through loyalty, caring, and love.

breed: To mate animals and help the offspring grow up.

communicate: To tell or pass on information.

congested: Crowded; a large amount of people and traffic.

distraction: Something that sidetracks a person or dog and makes them unable to pay attention.

foster parent: A person who cares for a child or a dog as a parent would by giving love, care, and a temporary home.

housebreak: To teach a puppy to go to the bathroom outdoors.

impaired: Something that is flawed, damaged, or injured.

independence: Freedom; to take care of oneself without any help.

interact: To talk with other people in a group.

mobility: The ability to move around safely.

obstacle: Something that blocks or stops someone from going ahead, such as a wall, fire hydrant, or ditch.

pedestrian: Someone who is walking.

residential: An area of homes or apartments where people live.

socialization: Training to take part in activities with many people around.

Organizations to Contact

American Council of the Blind (ACB)
1155 15th St. NW, Suite 1004
Washington, DC 20005
(800) 424-8666
www.acb.org
Founded in 1961, the ACB works for changes that improve life for people who are blind or have limited vision. The website describes the organization's purpose, publications, and services.

Guide Dog Foundation for the Blind
371 East Jericho Turnpike
Smithtown, NY 11787-2976
(800) 548-4337
www.guidedog.org
This is one of fourteen U.S. organizations that provides guide dogs to blind people worldwide. The group's website gives information about admissions, the breeding program, dormitories, kennels, training, and so on.

Guide Dogs for the Blind
P.O. Box 151200
San Rafael, CA 94915-1200
(800) 295-4050
www.guidedogs.com

This organization provides guide dogs and training to visually impaired people in the United States and Canada. The website has information on applying for training with a guide dog, agencies serving the blind, donations, events, graduate services, and raising a guide dog puppy.

Guide Dogs of America (GDA)
13445 Glenoaks Blvd.
Sylmar, CA 91342
(818) 362-5834
www.guidedogsofamerica.org
The GDA provides guide dogs and instruction for their use to blind and visually impaired people. The group's website offers information about these services and also about how people can volunteer for puppy raising.

The Seeing Eye
P.O. Box 375
Morristown, NJ 07963-0375
(973) 539-4425
www.seeingeye.org
Formed in 1929, this guide dog school serves qualified blind people throughout the United States and Canada. The website gives general information about laws and about traveling with a guide dog.

For Further Exploration

Caroline Arnold, *A Guide Dog Puppy Grows Up.* New York: Harcourt Brace Jovanovich, 1991. Follows the career of a guide dog from its raising as a puppy, through the training process, to placement with a blind person.

Charles and Linda George, *Guide Dogs.* New York: RiverFront Books, 1998. Describes the history of guide dogs, breeds of guide dogs, foster parents, formal training, and team training.

Susan Kuklin, *Mine for a Year.* New York: Coward-McCann, 1984. Describes a twelve-year-old boy's experience as a foster parent for a puppy that is destined to be trained as a guide dog.

Alice B. McGinty, *Guide Dogs.* New York: PowerKids Press, 1999. Describes the raising and training of Freedom, a seeing eye dog. It begins with Freedom's selection as a candidate up to its placement with a partner.

Index

Picture Credits

Cover photo: © Andy Levin, 1999/Photo
    Researchers, Inc.
© Bettmann/CORBIS, 8
© Cydney Conger/CORBIS, 32
© Tim Davis/Photo Researchers, Inc., 26
© Robert Dowling/CORBIS, 37
© Pat Doyle/CORBIS, 18
Toni and Ed Eames, 19, 38
© Spencer Grant/Photo Researchers, Inc., 25, 8
© Judy Griesedieck/CORBIS, 5
Guide Dog Foundation for the Blind, Inc., 6 (photo),
    10, 23, 27
© Richard Hutchings, 1979/Photo Researchers, Inc., 24
© L.A. Daily News/David Sprague, 20
© George Lepp/CORBIS, 21
© Andy Levin, 1999/Photo Researchers, Inc., 15
© Lawrence Migdale/Photo Researchers, Inc., 9
© William H. Mullins, 1998/Photo Researchers, Inc., 16
Lance Presnall, 7
Martha Schierholz, 6 (chart), 29, 36
© Peter Skinner/Photo Researchers, Inc., 13, 33
© Wartenberg/Picture Press/CORBIS, 35

About the Author

Judith Janda Presnall is an award-winning nonfiction writer. Her books include *Rachel Carson, Artificial Organs, The Giant Panda, Oprah Winfrey, Mount Rushmore, Life on Alcatraz, Animals That Glow, Animal Skeletons,* and *Circuses.* Presnall graduated from the University of Wisconsin in Whitewater. She is a recipient of the Jack London Award for meritorious service in the California Writers Club. She is also a member of the Society of Children's Book Writers and Illustrators. She lives in the Los Angeles area with her husband Lance.

YA 636.70886 PRESNALL
Presnall, Judith Janda.
Guide dogs /
shp   OCT   2006